Great Peace
for
Today

Other Books by Shirley D. Hicks

Great Peace for the Storms of Life

Great Peace for New Beginnings

Great Peace for Women

Great Peace for Mothers

Great Peace for Ministers

Great Peace for Men

Great Peace for Wives

Great Peace for Leaders

Great Peace for Using Your Gifts & Talents

and others...

See all of the books in the *Great Peace* series at
www.GreatPeace.com

Great Peace for Today

*How to Find Peace for Today
from People in the Bible*

SHIRLEY D. HICKS

Great Peace for Today

Copyright © 2017 by Shirley D. Hicks

Unless otherwise identified, Scripture quotations are taken from
the King James Version.

Scripture quotations noted NIV are from The Holy Bible, New
International Version® NIV®. Copyright © 1973, 1978, 1984,
2011 International Bible Society. Used by permission of
Zondervan. All rights reserved.

Scripture quotations noted NLT are from the *Holy Bible*, New
Living Translation, copyright © 1996, 2004. Used by permission
of Tyndale House Publishers, Inc., Wheaton, Illinois 60189.
All rights reserved.

Portions of this book have been adapted from *A Refuge from the
Storm*. Copyright © 1996, 1999 by Shirley D. Hicks.

ISBN 13: 978-1-947688-04-9

Great Peace Enterprises LLC
Alexandria, VA

www.GreatPeace.com

Dedicated
to every person who needs
peace for this day

Great peace have they which love thy law:
and nothing shall offend them.
Psalm 119:165

Contents

ACKNOWLEDGEMENTS

I would like to thank my Lord and Savior, Jesus Christ, for giving me this book and the opportunity to share it with people everywhere.

I would also like to thank my husband, Chris, and my daughter, Christen, for their love, support, and help in writing this book.

INTRODUCTION

It is the dawning of a new day. God has given you another day to live, learn, and grow. He wants you to enjoy this day because it is His gift to you. Today, He wants to give you His peace and help you endure the challenges you may be facing. He also wants to lead and guide you into the wonderful things He has for your life.

Great Peace for Today will help you discover the peace you can have every day when you apply God's word to your life. You may encounter tests and trials as you go through this day, but God can help you endure them, and show you how to fulfill your divine destiny. As you look into the lives of people in the Bible, you will see how God blessed them in the difficult times and directed them to the purposes and plans He had for their lives. You can apply the same biblical principles to your life today and live a life that is peaceful, rewarding, and fulfilling. This book will help you step into the pages of the Bible and find the peace you need today.

www.greatpeace.com

This is the day the LORD has made.
We will rejoice and be glad in it.
Psalm 118:24 (NLT)

GOD

God Is Calling You

Let the Lord be magnified,
which hath pleasure in the prosperity of his servant.
Psalm 35:27

God was planning to give the Israelites the best, even as they were arising out of the slavery in Egypt. The Egyptians treated them very harshly for many years. However, as the Israelites started their new journey to the Promise Land, they carried the best of Egypt with them. First, God gave them something that money could not buy – their freedom! Then He loaded them down with fine jewelry and clothes from their Egyptian neighbors.

In this new day, God is calling you to arise to His best for you. No matter what situation you may be facing, He is saying, "Arise!" Everything may not be perfect. You may even feel a little discouraged. However, God has you where you are for a reason. Perhaps He will load you down also with the best that this land has to offer as you arise by faith today. Listen as He calls you today.

In Your Life…

Do you believe God is calling you?
God has a purpose and a plan for everything that He allows in your life. He is using your situation to direct you into the calling that He has on your life. Listen for His voice. He is calling you to your divine purpose.

What is God calling you to do?
The still small voice that you hear in your heart is prompting you to do something specific for the Kingdom of God. Consider the gifts and talents that the Lord has given you. You can use them to bless your life, the lives of others, and the Kingdom of God.

How can you answer God's calling today?
Create a vision, develop a plan, and set goals to answer the calling that is upon your life. Today is a new opportunity to take steps in the direction of fulfilling your divine destiny. With faith in your heart, arise to answer God's call on your life. Isaiah 60:1 says, "Arise, shine; for thy light is come, and the glory of the LORD is risen upon thee." You must arise today.

Arise by faith today.

Arise

Arise, shine; for thy light is come,
and the glory of the LORD is risen upon thee.
Isaiah 60:1

When trouble and trials are all around,
The problems of life may knock you down,
And you may fall beneath life's care,
But God is saying you cannot stay there.
Though weeping may endure for a night,
God promised to make everything alright.
This is a new day, a brand new dawning,
He said that joy comes in the morning.

~

So lift up your head and open your eyes,
God is saying to you, "Arise!"
With faith in your heart, stand on your feet,
Get up and walk in your destiny.
The enemy wants to keep you down,
But do not be depressed and bound,

By satan's deceit and terrible lies,
When God is saying to you, "Arise!"

~

Arise, for God is extending His hand,
To lift you up and help you stand.
In Him is where your victory lies,
And He is saying to you, "Arise!"
He's lifting you up, can you feel it now?
He's saying, you must get up somehow,
For you have suffered long enough,
Now feel His love lifting you up.

~

Arise, for you are a child of the King,
Arise and go forth to do great things.
Arise and stir up the gifts in your soul,
Arise and achieve your God-given goals.
Arise and do what you must do,
Arise and make your dreams come true.
Now is your time, you must realize,
That God is saying to you, "Arise!"

Arise from fear, worry, and dread,
He's giving you beauty for ashes instead.
He's heard your prayers and your cries,
Today, He's saying to you, "Arise!"
Arise from pain, trouble, and strife,
Arise to walk in the newness of life.
Dry all of the tears from your eyes,
For God is saying to you, "Arise!"

~

Although trouble and trials are all around,
You cannot let them hold you down,
Give God your problems and your cares,
And the burdens that you cannot bear.
He is lifting you up out of the sod,
And standing you on the Word of God.
Believe in His word and reach for the prize,
For God is saying to you, "Arise!"

****

Promises for You

And I will see to it that the Egyptians load you down with gifts when you leave, so that you will by no means go out empty-handed! Every woman will ask for jewels, silver, gold, and the finest of clothes from her Egyptian master's wife and neighbors. You will clothe your sons and daughters with the best of Egypt!"

Exodus 3:21-22

Yet I am confident I will see the LORD's goodness while I am here in the land of the living.

Psalm 27:13 (NLT)

For his anger endureth but a moment; in his favour is life: weeping may endure for a night, but joy cometh in the morning.

Psalm 30:5

No good thing will he withhold from those who walk along his paths.

Psalms 84:11

The blessing of the Lord, it maketh rich.

Proverbs 10:22

Take possession of the land and settle in it, for I have given you the land to possess.

Numbers 33:53 (NIV)

Therefore I will look unto the LORD; I will wait for the God of my salvation: my God will hear me. Rejoice not against me, O mine enemy: when I fall, I shall arise; when I sit in darkness, the LORD shall be a light unto me.

Micah 7:7-8

Bless the LORD, O my soul: and all that is within me, bless his holy name. Bless the LORD, O my soul, and forget not all his benefits: Who forgiveth all thine iniquities; who healeth all thy diseases; Who redeemeth thy life from destruction; who crowneth thee with lovingkindness and tender mercies.

Psalm 103:1-4

Wherefore he saith, Awake thou that sleepest, and arise from the dead, and Christ shall give thee light.

Ephesians 5:14

For you bless the godly, O LORD; you surround them with your shield of love.

Psalm 5:12 (NLT)

Arise, for you are a child of the King,
Arise and go forth to do great things.

God Will Guide You

In all thy ways acknowledge him,
and he shall direct thy paths.
Proverbs 3:6

When you begin a new day, the road ahead may contain places of uncertainty and fear. You may not know which way to turn, or what decisions to make. This was the case in Abraham's life when God told him to leave his country and go to a land that He would show him. Abraham believed God for the new place, and God guided him to the land of Canaan. It was a rich and vast land with great blessings for Abraham and his posterity.

God has promised to guide you and prepare a path before you. He is always working behind the scenes to make a way for you. When God is your guide, the paths that were once crooked or impassable will become straight and easy. In Isaiah 42:16, God said, "These things will I do unto them, and not forsake them." Trust God to guide you to a blessed new day, and believe that He is always working for you behind the scenes.

In Your Life…

Do you need guidance today?
When you do not know what to do and which step to take next, ask God for guidance. Like Abraham, you may have to walk by faith, not knowing all of the answers. Eventually, you will make it to your Canaan Land.

Can you trust God's guidance?
Think about how God has divinely guided you in the past. In Psalm 32:8, He said "I will instruct thee and teach thee in the way which thou shalt go: I will guide thee with mine eye." Use those memories as the foundation for trusting His guidance today.

Can you see how God is working behind the scenes?
You may not understand all that God is doing in your life. However, He will send you some things in such unique ways that you will know it has to be from the hand of God. Trust Him when you cannot see or understand how He is working in your life. Believe that He is always working on your behalf behind the scenes of your life.

Believe God is working behind the scenes.

Behind the Scenes

For it is God which worketh in you
both to will and to do of his good pleasure.
Philippians 2:13

If you're in a trial you cannot understand,
If you can't see God's purpose or His plan,
And you don't know what it all means,
Believe God is working behind the scenes.
Behind the scenes, He does His best,
To give you strength for the trials and tests,
To give you peace in all of your labor,
To work things together in your favor.

~

Behind the scenes, He's working for you,
Doing the things only God can do,
Although, at times, He's misunderstood,
He's working it together for your good.
From behind the scenes, feel God's love,
And strength that only comes from above,
When you're burdened by life's routines,

Feel His love from behind the scenes.

~

He will give you a song out of the blue,
That strengthens and encourages you,
Or give you an idea that's timely and keen,
Because He is working behind the scenes.
If He blesses you and you're convinced,
That the blessing is no coincidence,
But you are not sure what it all means,
God is working behind the scenes.

~

When, finally, you get help that you need,
And what you've been trying now succeeds,
Or people are nice who were always mean,
God is working behind the scenes.
When doors open that were shut tight,
And you win the battles you couldn't fight,
When all the red lights suddenly turn green,
God is working behind the scenes.
So put thoughts of doubt out of your mind,

Because God is working all of the time,
Sending heavenly forces to intervene,
Doing His greatest work behind the scenes.
Don't worry about it, just be still,
He's working together His perfect will,
Arranging some things, moving others,
Adding one thing, subtracting another.

~

When all is over and you have victory,
He'll roll back the curtains and you will see,
Nothing just happens for the redeemed,
God is always working behind the scenes.
In the end, when the band plays your song,
You'll see God was working all along,
To give you a life beyond your dreams,
He's always working behind the scenes.

***

Promises for Guidance

And I will bring the blind by a way that they knew not; I will lead them in paths that they have not known: I will make darkness light before them, and crooked things straight. These things will I do unto them, and not forsake them.

Isaiah 42:16

I will instruct thee and teach thee in the way which thou shalt go: I will guide thee with mine eye.

Psalm 32:8

Thou shalt guide me with thy counsel, and afterward receive me to glory.

Psalm 73:24

Order my steps in thy word: and let not any iniquity have dominion over me.

Psalm 119:133

Without counsel purposes are disappointed: but in the multitude of counsellers they are established.

Proverbs 15:22

18

Call unto me, and I will answer thee, and shew thee great and mighty things, which thou knowest not.

Jeremiah 33:3

Teach me thy way, O LORD; I will walk in thy truth: unite my heart to fear thy name.

Psalm 86:11

But the path of the just *is* as the shining light, that shineth more and more unto the perfect day.

Proverbs 4:18

For this God *is* our God for ever and ever: he will be our guide *even* unto death.

Psalm 48:14

But when he, the Spirit of truth, comes, he will guide you into all the truth. He will not speak on his own; he will speak only what he hears, and he will tell you what is yet to come.

John 16:13 (NIV)

For as many as are led by the Spirit of God, they are the sons of God.

Romans 8:14

19

Behind the scenes, He's working for you,
Doing the things only God can do.

God Understands

*For your Father knoweth what things
ye have need of, before ye ask him.
Matthew 6:8*

As the Israelites travelled to the Promise
Land, God chose the best route for them to
take. He was mindful of how they were
feeling as they started out on the difficult
journey. The most direct route through the
land of the Philistines was not the best route
for them. Instead, He led them by the way of
the Red Sea wilderness. He gave them a cloud
during the day to protect them from the
desert heat, and a pillar of fire during the
night to give them light and warmth.

As you begin this new day, God
understands how you feel. He is planning the
best route for you to take to reach your new
goal. His word will lead you by day and guide
you by night so that you will be able to travel
on life's journey without fear, doubt, and
unbelief. No matter what you face along this
route for your life, allow God to lead you, and
remember that He understands how you feel.

In Your Life...

Are you feeling tired and discouraged?
As a Christian, you are in a spiritual battle. At times, you may become tired and discouraged. However, that is not a time to quit. Ask the Lord for strength and continue to fight the good fight of faith. You can have victory through Jesus Christ if you persevere.

In what way is God reassuring you of His presence?
God understands how you feel and He will send you something to reassure you of His presence. You may hear a song or a message that encourages you. A Bible verse may come to your mind that speaks directly to your situation. God will find a way to reassure you of His presence.

What things can you do to stay encouraged?
You can stay encouraged by reading God's word. Romans 10:17 says, "Faith cometh by hearing, and hearing by the word of God." Read the Bible to strengthen your faith. You will see that Jesus experienced life as you do today. He understands how you feel.

Jesus understands how you feel.

Jesus Understands

For we have not an high priest which cannot be touched with the feeling of our infirmities; but was in all points tempted like as we are, yet without sin.
Hebrews 4:15

As you juggle all of life demands,

You may wonder if Jesus understands.

Does He understand how you feel?

Is His love for you genuine and real?

Can He understand the problems you face?

And what it's like to be in your place?

~

Yes, Jesus really does understand,

For He lived and dwelled among man,

He realizes the situation you're in,

And all of the feelings you have within.

Jesus came and lived a humble life,

Although He was the anointed Christ.

He was also human. He worked and slept,

And when He was sad, Jesus wept.

He was tempted like you, again and again,

He faced trouble, hatred, and pain,

He understands your concerns and needs,

He is touched by the feelings of your
infirmities.

But all of life's challenges, He overcame,

And with His help, you can do the same.

So as you juggle your life's demands,

Always remember that Jesus understands.

****

Promises for Understanding

In the world ye shall have tribulation: but be of good cheer; I have overcome the world.

John 16:33

For your Father knoweth what things ye have need of, before ye ask him.

Matthew 6:8

He took not away the pillar of the cloud by day, nor the pillar of fire by night, from before the people.

Exodus 13:22

Thou shalt not be affrighted at them: for the Lord thy God is among you, a mighty God and terrible.

Deuteronomy 7:21

Are not five sparrows sold for two farthings, and not one of them is forgotten before God? But even the very hairs of your head are all numbered. Fear not therefore: ye are of more value than many sparrows.

Luke 12:6-7

This High Priest of ours understands our weaknesses, for he faced all of the same testings we do, yet he did not sin.

Hebrews 4:15 (NLT)

If thou shalt say in thine heart, These nations are more than I; how can I dispossess them? Thou shalt not be afraid of them: but shalt well remember what the Lord thy God did unto Pharaoh, and unto all Egypt.

Deuteronomy 7:17-19

Only fear the LORD, and serve him in truth with all your heart: for consider how great things he hath done for you.

1 Samuel 12:24

And therefore will the LORD wait, that he may be gracious unto you, and therefore will he be exalted, that he may have mercy upon you: for the LORD is a God of judgment: blessed are all they that wait for him.

Isaiah 30:18

He heals the brokenhearted and bandages their wounds.

Psalm 147:3 (NLT)

As you juggle your life's demands,
Always remember that Jesus understands.

JUST

Just Depend on Him

*He giveth power to the faint;
and to them that have no might he increaseth strength.
Isaiah 40:29*

Sometimes situations in life tend to get worse right before they get better. This was the case when Moses and Aaron told the Israelites that their deliverance from slavery was imminent. Soon afterwards, Pharaoh dashed their hopes by instructing the taskmasters to give them more work than they could possibly do. The people blamed Moses and Aaron for making their lives worse, and would not listen to them anymore. However, God used the situation to teach them how to depend on Him and to show them His mighty power.

As you begin this new day, you may also face harsh conditions and situations that are beyond your control. Just remember to depend on God. It is often darkest before dawn. Hold to His promises, despite what is happening in your life. Perhaps God is showing you that you can depend on Him, and He will reveal to you His mighty power.

29

In Your Life…

Are you facing harsh conditions?
You may be experiencing some harsh conditions that are unavoidable. Life will unleash times of pain, heartache, and struggle. Yet, Jesus promised to never leave you, nor forsake you. He will help you endure the tough times.

How can you depend on God?
You can depend on God by trusting His word. By reading the Bible, you can learn to trust God by seeing how He worked in the lives of other people and believe that He can do the same for you when you obey Him and believe. Begin to read the Bible every day.

Is God revealing His mighty power to you?
Look at your life today. Think about the ways in which God is showing you that He is a mighty and powerful God. Consider your answered prayers. Reflect on the wonderful things that happened in your life that were not coincidences. They were things that only a big God could have made happen in your life.

You serve a great big God.

A Great Big God

For the LORD is a great God,
and a great King above all gods.
Psalm 95:3

Today, do you have a big problem to solve?
Make sure you have your big God involved.
For God is your refuge and your strength,
And He will go through very great lengths,
To answer your prayers and hear your cry,
So, don't be sad and keep asking why,
Why this big problem and why this big test,
When I've tried hard to do my very best?

~

But life will contain some aggravations,
And Jesus said you would have tribulations.
Yes, trials and tests will come your way,
And you may see some very dark days.
But God is with you as problems evolve,
Your load to carry, your problems to solve.
If they are too great and too big for you,

31

You serve a God who is big and great too.
When your situation is difficult and tough,
He is a great God who is big enough,
To help you get through them and escape,
The snare of the enemy, for God is great!

~

In greatness, He gave Moses true victory,
As Pharaoh's army drowned in the sea.
In greatness, He helped David alone,
To slay Goliath with a sling and a stone.
In greatness, He gave Elijah rain in the sky,
When the land was famished and very dry.
In greatness, He sent His only son,
To redeem mankind from the evil one.

~

In greatness, Jesus came for you and me,
To heal, and deliver, and set men free.
In greatness, Jesus died on the cross,
And those who trust Him will not be lost.

~

In greatness, He can deliver you,
From the problems you are going through.
For whatever problems that life may bring,
Your God is a great and mighty king.

~

Live by His words, keep His commands,
Even when you do not understand.
Hold to His promises and always pray,
Let Him handle your problems His way.
He will bless you if you trust Him and wait,
Because He is a God who is big and great.

****

Promises for Dependence

Why art thou cast down, O my soul? and why art thou disquieted within me? hope thou in God: for I shall yet praise him, who is the health of my countenance, and my God.

Psalm 42:11

...before honour is humility.

Proverbs 15:33

For a just man falleth seven times, and riseth up again: but the wicked shall fall into mischief.

Proverbs 24:16

The LORD upholdeth all that fall, and raiseth up all those that be bowed down.

Psalm 145:14

For his anger endureth but a moment; in his favour is life: weeping may endure for a night, but joy cometh in the morning.

Psalm 30:5

And let us not be weary in well doing: for in due season we shall reap, if we faint not.

Galatians 6:9

The house of the wicked shall be overthrown: but the tabernacle of the upright shall flourish.

Proverbs 14:11

Thou shalt arise, and have mercy upon Zion: for the time to favour her, yea, the set time, is come.

Psalm 102:13

The Lord is not slack concerning his promise, as some men count slackness; but is longsuffering to us-ward, not willing that any should perish, but that all should come to repentance.

2 Peter 3:9

Behold, the LORD'S hand is not shortened, that it cannot save; neither his ear heavy, that it cannot hear.

Isaiah 59:1

The salvation of the righteous comes from the LORD; he is their stronghold in time of trouble. The LORD helps them and delivers them; he delivers them from the wicked.

Psalm 37:39-40 (NIV)

But God is with you as problems evolve,
Your load to carry, your problems to solve.

Just Trust Him

And thou shalt know that I am the LORD:
for they shall not be ashamed that wait for me.
Isaiah 49:23

God promised to give Abraham and Sarah a child, but it did not happen right away. In their impatience, they decided to take matters into their own hands, which led to a terrible mistake. Later, God blessed them to have a son named Isaac in their old age. By that time, they were extremely grateful, had much more wisdom, and great wealth. Perhaps Abraham could offer Isaac the stability that he did not have earlier in his life. It was worth the wait.

Sometimes you may have to trust God's timing, but when He finally blesses you, it will be worth the wait. What is God planning for you that is worth the wait? When you grow tired, or feel like He is never going to answer your prayers, consider Abraham and Sarah. Think of all the benefits they gained by waiting on God. Wait on God and trust His timing. If you do, He will also bless you. Then, you will see and understand that it was all worth the wait.

In Your Life…

For what blessings are you praying?
Surely, you have a desire in your heart of something you want God to do for you. After you pray and believe, trust His timing, no matter how long it takes. He is able to bless you, but it will be in His way and according to His plan for your life.

Why should you trust God?
God can see the beginning and the ending of your circumstance, whereas you can only see this day. If you wait on His timing, you can avoid making mistakes that you may regret for many years to come. God knows what is best for you in every situation, and some things will simply take time.

How can God bless you immediately?
Jesus blessed many people who had been in dire situations for a long time. Each person demonstrated that waiting on God may be difficult and trying, but when He finally steps in, things can change very quickly and amazingly.

Jesus can bless you immediately.

Immediately

So do not throw away your confidence;
it will be richly rewarded.
Hebrews 10:35 (NIV)

Whatever you're going through today,

Do not throw your confidence away.

You may have suffered for a long time,

But Jesus still has you on His mind.

For the Bible says, and it's plain to see,

That Jesus did some things immediately.

It really didn't matter how long it had been,

Everything changed when Jesus stepped in.

~

For in the Bible, we can find,

People who had waited a very long time,

For God to deliver and set them free,

But then, one day, immediately,

A lame man began to walk,

A dumb man began to talk,

A blind man began to see,

39

Jesus did some things immediately.

~

Immediately He raised the dead,
Immediately is what the Bible said.
Immediately the widow of Nain,
Received her son alive again.

~

Immediately, after eighteen years,
A woman was loosed from pain and tears.

~

Immediately He took clay from the ground,
And turned a blind man's life around.

~

Immediately a demon-filled man,
Was freed by the power in Jesus' hand.
After Jesus cast the demons into the swine,
The man sat clothed and in his right mind.

~

For thirty-eight years a man was lame,
But immediately healed when Jesus came.

~

At a wedding in Cana, in a time of need,
He turned water into wine immediately.

~

A woman with an issue of blood was free,
Of her terrible disease immediately.

~

And immediately the winds ceased,
On the stormy sea when He said "Peace!"

~

So, in your situation, could it be,
That Jesus will change it immediately?
Sometimes when you've suffered long,
You may feel as if all hope is gone,
And the way out, you cannot see,
But Jesus can come and immediately,
Touch your situation and instantly bring,
A miracle that changes everything.

~

Immediately He can change your life,
He's the Son of God, He is the Christ.

41

So, whatever you're going through today,
Don't throw your confidence away.
It doesn't matter how long it's been,
Everything changes when Jesus steps in.

~

Pray about what you want Him to do,
Immediately, especially for you.
Then trust in Him and allow Him to be,
A God who works immediately.

****

Promises for Trusting

Now unto him that is able to do exceeding abundantly above all that we ask or think, according to the power that worketh in us.

Ephesians 3:20

And God is able to make all grace abound toward you; that ye, always having all sufficiency in all things, may abound to every good work.

2 Corinthians 9:8

For the LORD is a God of judgment: blessed are all they that wait for him.

Isaiah 30:18

I will call on the LORD, who is worthy to be praised: so shall I be saved from mine enemies.

2 Samuel 22:4

Thou shalt arise, and have mercy upon Zion: for the time to favour her, yea, the set time, is come.

Psalm 102:13

Know therefore that the LORD your God is God; he is the faithful God, keeping his covenant of love to a thousand generations of those who love him and keep his commandments.

Deuteronomy 7:9 (NIV)

Praise ye the LORD. Blessed is the man that feareth the LORD, that delighteth greatly in his commandments.

Psalm 112:1

He will not forsake thee, neither destroy thee, nor forget the covenant of thy fathers which he sware unto them.

Deuteronomy 4:9

But they that wait upon the LORD shall renew their strength; they shall mount up with wings as eagles; they shall run, and not be weary; and they shall walk, and not faint.

Isaiah 40:31

I had fainted, unless I had believed to see the goodness of the LORD in the land of the living. Wait on the LORD: be of good courage, and he shall strengthen thine heart.

Psalm 27:13-14

Immediately He can change your life,
He is the Son of God, He is the Christ.

Just Honor Him

*I will pay thee my vows, which my lips have uttered,
and my mouth hath spoken, when I was in trouble.
Psalm 66:14*

When you are going through a difficult time in your life, you may sincerely make a promise to the Lord. You might promise Him something that you will do for Him if He would only fulfill a request that you have. Have you ever made a promise to God like that? How important is it to Him that you keep your promise? God is faithful to His promises to you, and you should also be faithful to your promises to Him.

In Ecclesiastes 5, the writer reminds us that we should always keep our promises to God. We should be mindful of the things we have promised the Lord and be determined to fulfill them. Yes, God is merciful, forgiving, and full of grace, but do not take advantage of His kindness to you in any area of your life. Be faithful and keep your promises to Him. Honor the vow that you have made to Him.

In Your Life…

Have you made any promises to God?
Think about the things that you promised God when you were in a desperate situation. Have you done them? If not, consider ways in which you can work towards fulfilling them today. You may have to start in small ways and develop a plan to accomplish the goal.

How long has it been since you made the promise?
You may be thinking that you will fulfil the vow "one day." One day may become one week, one year, or one decade. Do not put it off any longer. While it is true that God is patience, the time to fulfil your vow is now.

What if you do not fulfil your vow?
If you do not fulfil your vow, then God understands – He understands that you made a promise that you did not keep. God said in Deuteronomy 23:21, "When you make a vow to the LORD your God, be prompt in fulfilling whatever you promised him." Find a way to fulfil the vow you made to the Lord.

Fulfil your promises to God.

Honor Your Vow

When you make a vow to the LORD your God, be prompt in fulfilling whatever you promised him. For the LORD your God demands that you promptly fulfill all your vows, or you will be guilty of sin.
Deuteronomy 23:21 (NLT)

Did you make a promise to the Lord one day,
About what you would do if He made a way?
Did you make a vow to Him about,
What you would do if He brought you out?

~

But after He heard and answered you,
Did you do what you said you would do?
If you have not yet honored your vow,
This is the time to do it now.

~

Yes, this is the time, you must go ahead,
And do for God what you sincerely said,
The promise you made with such great care,
That you would do if He heard your prayer.

He's done His part, He's made the way,
Fulfill your promise and don't delay.

~

God has not forgotten, He's waiting on you,
To do the thing you promised to do.
So, find a way to do it somehow,
Do what you said and honor your vow.

****

Promises for Vows

However, it is not a sin to refrain from making a vow. But once you have voluntarily made a vow, be careful to fulfill your promise to the LORD your God.

Deuteronomy 23:22-23 (NLT)

A man who makes a vow to the LORD or makes a pledge under oath must never break it. He must do exactly what he said he would do.

Numbers 30:2 (NLT)

When thou vowest a vow unto God, defer not to pay it; for *he hath* no pleasure in fools: pay that which thou hast vowed.

Ecclesiastes 5:4

What mighty praise, O God, belongs to you in Zion. We will fulfill our vows to you, for you answer our prayers. All of us must come to you.

Psalm 65:1-2 (NLT)

It is better not to make a vow than to make one and not fulfill it.

Ecclesiastes 5:4

This is what the LORD commands: When a man makes a vow to the LORD or takes an oath to obligate himself by a pledge, he must not break his word but must do everything he said.

Numbers 30:1-2 (NIV)

Then Jacob made this vow: "If God will indeed be with me and protect me on this journey, and if he will provide me with food and clothing, and if I return safely to my father's home, then the LORD will certainly be my God."

Genesis 28:20-21 (NLT)

In her deep anguish Hannah prayed to the LORD, weeping bitterly. And she made a vow, saying, "LORD Almighty, if you will only look on your servant's misery and remember me, and not forget your servant but give her a son, then I will give him to the LORD for all the days of his life."

1 Samuel 1:10-11 (NIV)

LORD, remember David, *and* all his afflictions: How he sware unto the LORD, *and* vowed unto the mighty *God* of Jacob.

Psalm 132:1-2

If you have not yet honored your vow,
This is the time to do it now.

KEEP

Keep Looking Up

*Looking unto Jesus
the author and finisher of our faith.
Hebrews 12:2*

Throughout the Bible, God worked in the lives of His people in awesome ways. He used ordinary people to fulfill His divine plans and purposes. Yes, people just like you. Still today, you can see God's mighty hand at work in the lives of His people, and in your life as well.

Keep looking up to Jesus for everything you need to make it through this day that He has given you. If you are facing a painful or difficult situation, you must keep looking up. Sometimes He will demonstrate His mighty power in your life by sending miracles to deliver, heal, and help you overcome the obstacles that you face. Yet, at other times, He may choose to send you the miracle of His presence and His grace to help you bear the trials. In whatever way He chooses to bless you, you can still feel His love, see His grace, and know that He really is an awesome God who loves you very much.

In Your Life…

What miracle has God given you in your life?
The miracles of God are not just for the Bible. He will also send you a miracle in your life just when you need it most. When God answers your prayers in amazing ways, it is not just chance or luck. God is at work in your life.

How does God make His presence known to you?
You can sense the presence of God in your own unique way. He may speak quietly to your heart, through a scripture, in a song, or in some other special way. In whatever way He chooses to make Himself known to you, you will sense the Lord's presence.

Will you trust Him to use your pain and hurts?
God will not always send miracles to answer all of your prayers. Sometimes He will give you the strength to go through the difficult times. When God does not answer your prayers in the way you think He should, you still must trust Him. Trust Him to use your pain and hurts for His glory and your good.

Sometimes God works in a different way.

Sometimes God

For with God all things are possible
Mark 10:27

Sometimes God gives us miracles from above,

To show us His power, to show us His love.

He may do unusual and different things,

Like when David killed Goliath with a sling.

When others were using swords and shields,

God drew the young boy from the fields,

And slew the giant with a stone and sling,

Then made the shepherd boy a great king.

~

We may not fathom nor understand,

The power and wonder of God's hand.

He leaves us in wonder, totally awed,

But after all, He really is a great God,

Omnipotent, omniscience, faithful, and true,

And nothing is impossible for God to do.

~

When our pain is great and our pain is deep,
He arises, it seems, as out of His sleep,
And saves us, delivers us, heals our diseases,
He displays His power however He pleases.

~

Other times, the miracle is having Him there,
To love and support us, and simply to care,
To comfort and guide us, to just understand,
To walk beside us and hold our hands.

~

For sometimes He uses our pain and hurts,
To bless, inspire, and encourage His church.
And only God can take one person's pain,
And bless His church over and over again.
That is also a miracle sent from above,
And we still see His power and feel His love!

****

Promises for Looking Up

Looking unto Jesus the author and finisher of *our* faith; who for the joy that was set before him endured the cross, despising the shame, and is set down at the right hand of the throne of God.

Hebrews 12:2

Look upon mine affliction and my pain; and forgive all my sins.

Psalm 25:18

And God shall wipe all tears from their eyes; and there shall be no more death, neither sorrow, nor crying, neither shall there be any more pain: for the former things are passed away.

Revelation 21:4

And Jesus went forth, and saw a great multitude, and was moved with compassion toward them, and he healed their sick.

Matthew 14:14

For I will restore health unto thee, and I will heal thee of thy wounds, saith the Lord.

Jeremiah 30:17

And the whole multitude sought to touch him: for there went virtue out of him, and healed them all.

Luke 6:19

And God is able to make all grace abound toward you; that ye, always having all sufficiency in all things, may abound to every good work.

2 Corinthians 9:8

Behold, I will bring it health and cure, and I will cure them, and will reveal unto them the abundance of peace and truth.

Jeremiah 33:6

But he was wounded for our transgressions, he was bruised for our iniquities: the chastisement of our peace was upon him; and with his stripes we are healed.

Isaiah 53:5

He sent his word, and healed them, and delivered them from their destructions.

Psalm 107:20

Sometimes He uses our pain and hurts,
To bless and encourage His church.

Keep Holding On

*Timothy, my son, I am giving you this command
in keeping with the prophecies once made about you,
so that by recalling them you may fight the battle well,
holding on to faith and a good conscience.*
1 Timothy 1:18-19 (NIV)

David was just a young shepherd boy when God drew him out of the fields and used him to win a mighty battle. Later, God made him a king over all Israel. It was an awesome demonstration of the love and power of God in a young man's life. David had many battles to fight in His life. He won some of the battles and he lost some of them. In the end, he was victorious in his walk with the Lord.

As you begin your day, you may also face many battles. If you find yourself bending beneath a load of care, remember that you must keep holding on to the promises of God, despite what happens in your life. Do not lose confidence in His word. In the end, you will be victorious in your walk with the Lord if you bend, but do not break.

In Your Life...

What battles are you facing today?
As a Christian, you are in a spiritual war and you will have battles to fight. You will experience the trials and difficulties of life, but you have God almighty fighting for you. With His divine help, you can be victorious in the battles you face.

Can God use your victories?
God can use your victories to strengthen your faith in Him. He can also use them to encourage others who may be going through similar situations. The testimonies that you share will bless and inspire them to hold on.

Can God use your defeats?
In similar ways, God can use your defeats to show you that you must depend on Him for everything you need. He can also use them to show others that we all have to fight the lust of the flesh, the lust of the eye, and the pride of life. Through it all, He will give you a testimony that His love, grace, and mercy is great for everyone who will keep holding on.

If you bend beneath care, do not break.

Bend and Not Break

Now unto him that is able to keep you from falling,
and to present you faultless before the presence of his
glory with exceeding joy.
Jude 1:24

The winds of adversity are blowing my way,

And I face a new challenge every day.

I say to my soul, "My faith may be shaken,

But, oh my soul, do not be mistaken.

~

God is on my side in this adversity,

And this I know - My God is for me.

No weapon formed against me will win,

God is the one on whom I depend.

~

The wind is strong, but too much is at stake,

I may have to bend, but I will not break.

I may bend beneath trouble and care,

I may bend beneath things that are unfair.

I may bend beneath all of my mistakes,

63

I may bend beneath pain, but I will not break.

~

Because Jesus loves me and one day I'll see,

That He's only planning His best for me.

In this situation, I will do what it takes,

I am determined to bend but not break."

****

Promises for Holding On

O Lord, you are so good, so ready to forgive, so full of unfailing love for all who ask for your help. Listen closely to my prayer, O LORD; hear my urgent cry. I will call to you whenever I'm in trouble, and you will answer me.

Psalm 86:5-7 (NLT)

And all things, whatsoever ye shall ask in prayer, believing, ye shall receive.

Matthew 21:22

The LORD says, "I will rescue those who love me. I will protect those who trust in my name. When they call on me, I will answer; I will be with them in trouble. I will rescue and honor them."

Psalm 91:14-15 (NLT)

Don't worry about anything; instead, pray about everything. Tell God what you need, and thank him for all he has done. Then you will experience God's peace, which exceeds anything we can understand. His peace will guard your hearts and minds as you live in Christ Jesus.

Philippians 4:6-7 (NLT)

This is the confidence we have in approaching God: that if we ask anything according to his will, he hears us. And if we know that he hears us—whatever we ask—we know that we have what we asked of him.

1 John 5:14-15 (NIV)

Call unto me, and I will answer thee, and shew thee great and mighty things, which thou knowest not.

Jeremiah 33:3

Are any of you suffering hardships? You should pray. Are any of you happy? You should sing praises. Are any of you sick? You should call for the elders of the church to come and pray over you, anointing you with oil in the name of the Lord. Such a prayer offered in faith will heal the sick, and the Lord will make you well.

James 5:13-15 (NLT)

Humble yourselves, therefore, under God's mighty hand, that he may lift you up in due time. Cast all your anxiety on him because he cares for you.

1 Peter 5:6-7 (NIV)

God is on my side in this adversity,
And this I know - My God is for me.

Keep Praising Him

*For what you have done I will always praise you in the
presence of your faithful people. And I will hope in
your name, for your name is good.*
Psalm 52:9 (NIV)

Moses told the Israelites that they should
always remember the day that the Lord
brought them out of Egypt with His mighty
miracles. Later, he told them to teach their
children and grandchildren about what the
Lord had done for them. They also set aside
special days to celebrate God's blessings, and
some of them are still celebrated today.

You will experience some things that
you should always remember. God wants you
to remember the great things He has done for
you. When He delivers you or does something
extraordinary in your life, praise God always
for His love and blessings in your life. God
has been very good to you. Always remember
the things He brought you through and keep
praising Him for His goodness.

In Your Life...

For what things should you praise God?
You should praise God for His goodness in your life. You should also praise Him for the blessings that He has given you throughout your life. Also, praise Him because He is God, the creator of the entire universe.

Why is praise important to you?
Praising God will give you joy, hope, strength, and encouragement for today. It also gives you the opportunity to verbalize God's greatness. You may think about it in your mind and feel it in your heart, but praise gives you the opportunity to actually say it.

In what ways can you praise God?
In Psalm 150, David wrote about the many different ways in which you can praise God. You can praise God with words of honor and devotion, in a song, on an instrument, or even in a dance. Find a way to praise God and demonstrate the love, trust, and reverence that you have in your heart for Him today.

The Lord is worthy to be praised.

Keep Praising the Lord

This day is holy to our Lord.
Do not grieve, for the joy of the LORD is your
strength.
Nehemiah 8:10 (NIV)

Problems will come in so many ways,

But don't let them stop or hinder your praise.

When your day is dark or your night is long,

Open your mouth and start singing a song.

The Lord is powerful and mighty to save,

And this is the day that the Lord has made.

Tell sadness and sorrow they must depart,

And praise God with a song from your heart.

~

Your song may be short or of a great length,

But the joy of the Lord will be your strength.

Keep praising Him, you will not be the same,

When you lift your voice and praise His name.

Sing Him a sweet song, make a joyful sound,

When praises go up, blessings come down.

So praise Him regardless of how you may feel,
Praise Him because you know He is real.
Praise Him for all the good He has done,
Praise Him for the battles you have won.
Praise Him for being your strength and guide,
Praise Him for walking by your side.

~

Praise Him when you don't know what to do,
Praise Him for all He's brought you through.
Praise Him when you don't understand,
Praise Him because you are in His hands.
Praise Him every time you get a chance,
Praise Him in a song, or even a dance.

~

Because problems will come in so many ways,
But don't let them stop or hinder your praise.
Just sing a sweet song, strike up a chord,
Lift your voice and keep praising the Lord.

****

Promises for Praising God

I will bless the LORD at all times: his praise shall continually be in my mouth. My soul shall make her boast in the LORD: the humble shall hear thereof, and be glad.

Psalm 34:1-3

And Miriam the prophetess, the sister of Aaron, took a timbrel in her hand; and all the women went out after her with timbrels and with dances.

Exodus 15:20

Speaking to yourselves in psalms and hymns and spiritual songs, singing and making melody in your heart to the Lord; Giving thanks always for all things unto God and the Father in the name of our Lord Jesus Christ.

Ephesians 5:19-20

Praise the LORD. Praise God in his sanctuary; praise him in his mighty heavens. Praise him for his acts of power; praise him for his surpassing greatness.

Psalm 150:1-2 (NIV)

O LORD, thou art my God; I will exalt thee, I will praise thy name; for thou hast done wonderful things; thy counsels of old are faithfulness and truth.

Isaiah 25:1

Therefore, let us offer through Jesus a continual sacrifice of praise to God, proclaiming our allegiance to his name.

Hebrews 13:15 (NLT)

Praise the LORD! How good to sing praises to our God! How delightful and how fitting!

Psalm 147:1 (NLT)

Praise the LORD! Praise the LORD from the heavens! Praise him from the skies! Praise him, all his angels! Praise him, all the armies of heaven! Praise him, sun and moon! Praise him, all you twinkling stars! Praise him, skies above! Praise him, vapors high above the clouds! Let every created thing give praise to the LORD, for he issued his command, and they came into being.

Psalm 148:1-5 (NLT)

Whoso offereth praise glorifieth me.

Psalm 50:23

Praise Him every time you get a chance,
Praise Him in a song, or even a dance.

BE

Be Generous

Give, and it shall be given unto you.
Luke 6:38

In Luke 6:38, Jesus taught His disciples the importance of giving. He said, "Give, and it shall be given unto you; good measure, pressed down, and shaken together, and running over, shall men give into your bosom. For with the same measure that ye mete withal it shall be measured to you again." Jesus taught them that giving is not only a blessing to the receiver, but it will also be a blessing to you. In God's time, your giving will be reciprocated in your life. In the same way that you give, others will give unto you.

In your relationship with the Lord, put Him first in every aspect of your life, including your giving. When you give generously to God's work, you will have favor with an awesome God who owns both Heaven and earth. As you are beginning this new day, be generous and honor God in your giving. When you give to God and to men, blessings will abound in your life.

In Your Life…

Are you giving to God?
Honor the Lord by giving back to the Kingdom of God. Jesus said in Luke 6:38, "Give, and it shall be given unto you." Giving is a direct result of receiving. Make sure you give to God first, and He will bless your life.

Are you giving to others?
Giving to others in need is also important. Pray and ask the Lord to show you something that you share with someone else. What you may consider as insignificant may be the answer to someone else's prayers.

Are you giving cheerfully?
God not only wants you to give, but to give willingly and cheerfully. An old adage says, "You can't beat God's giving." When you are a blessing to the Kingdom of God, He will surely bless you in return. So be happy when you have the opportunity to give unto the Lord. When you do, you are funding God's work, and He will supply the things that you need in your life today.

Give to God cheerfully.

A Cheerful Giver

For God loveth a cheerful giver.
2 Corinthians 9:7

The Bible says God loves cheerful giving,
It is such an important part of living,
When you give to God and to man,
He will bless you over and over again.

~

Your life will be blessed and not cursed,
When you honor God and give to him first.
According to Malachi three, verse ten,
Windows of Heaven will open, my friend,
And God will bless you from on high,
With some things that money cannot buy.

~

He'll rebuke the devourer for your sake,
And help you avoid costly mistakes.
He'll bless your work and livelihood too,
And many more things God will do.
You won't have room enough to receive it,

78

Blessings so great, you will not believe it.

~

And in Luke Chapter 6, verse 38,
The Bible says giving to others is great.
Give to others, and they will give to you,
Blessings pressed down, running over too.

~

So do not worry when times are tough,
For givers will always have enough.
Just give unto God and unto man,
And you will be blessed again and again.

****

Promises for Generosity

Every man according as he purposeth in his heart, so let him give; not grudgingly, or of necessity: for God loveth a cheerful giver.

2 Corinthians 9:7

Give, and it shall be given unto you; good measure, pressed down, and shaken together, and running over, shall men give into your bosom.

Luke 6:38

Give to those who ask, and don't turn away from those who want to borrow.

Matthew 5:42 (NLT)

The liberal soul shall be made fat: and he that watereth shall be watered also himself.

Proverbs 11:25

Bring ye all the tithes into the storehouse, that there may be meat in mine house, and prove me now herewith, saith the Lord of hosts, if I will not open you the windows of heaven, and pour you out a blessing, that there shall not be room enough to receive it.

Malachi 3:10

And all these blessings shall come on thee, and overtake thee, if thou shalt hearken unto the voice of the LORD thy God.

Deuteronomy 28:2

The blessing of the Lord, it maketh rich, and he addeth no sorrow with it.

Proverbs 10:22

A good man leaveth an inheritance to his children's children: and the wealth of the sinner is laid up for the just.

Proverbs 13:22

For he satisfieth the longing soul, and filleth the hungry soul with goodness.

Psalm 107:9

No good thing will he withhold from them that walk uprightly.

Psalm 84:11

And if you give even a cup of cold water to one of the least of my followers, you will surely be rewarded.

Matthew 10:42 (NLT)

The Bible says God loves cheerful giving,
It is such an important part of living.

Be Prayerful

Pray without ceasing.
1 Thessalonians 5:17

Prayer is one of the most important parts of maintaining a good relationship with God. As you begin this new day, you must begin with prayer. No great accomplishments for God are ever successful without prayer. In fact, Jesus said in Luke 18:1 that we should always pray and never give up.

Jesus showed us the importance of prayer. He often prayed early in the morning before starting His day, and late at night at the end of His day. Luke 6:12 tells us that Jesus prayed all night before choosing His disciples. His prayer life gave Him strength in His daily walk and the power to bless and help others. If prayer was important to Jesus, shouldn't it be very important to you also? Fill your day with prayer. Your walk with the Lord and your prayers can influence someone else's life. Never become too busy to pray, because the situation you are facing today may not be just for you. Perhaps God will bless others also.

In Your Life...

Is prayer a priority in your life?
Get up each morning and begin your day with prayer. This is another way that you can keep God first in your life – by honoring Him with your time. It will also help prepare you to face this day in the strength and joy of the Lord.

Can your prayers really help you?
Prayer works. Jesus said in Matthew 7:7 (NLT), "Keep on asking, and you will receive what you ask for. Keep on seeking, and you will find. Keep on knocking, and the door will be opened to you."

Can your prayers really help others?
Your prayers can be a blessing to you and to others. Paul said in Ephesians 6:18 (NLT) that we should "Pray in the Spirit at all times and on every occasion. Stay alert and be persistent in your prayers for all believers everywhere." Every believer is in a spiritual battle. When you pray for others, you can help them in the battles they are facing.

Your trials may be for others too.

Not Just for You

And at midnight Paul and Silas prayed,
and sang praises unto God: and the prisoners heard
them.
And suddenly there was a great earthquake, so that
the foundations of the prison were shaken: and
immediately all the doors were opened, and every one's
bands were loosed.
Acts 16:25-26

Think about what you are going through,

Your problems may not be just for you.

People are hurting and only God knows,

That some situations must be exposed.

He may send you in places of misery,

To help others who need to be free.

~

Like Paul and Silas who were placed in Jail,

And it seemed like their prayers had failed.

Their imprisonment was cruel and unfair,

But in that place, other people were there,

Who were bound with chains and rods,

Who did not know about the Son of God.
But when Paul and Silas sang and prayed,
Everyone's chains were loosened that day.
The jailer didn't know exactly what to do,
But with their help, he was saved too.
God sent them there, in a place so strange,
To help bring about a miraculous change.

~

Where is the place that God has sent you,
And what is He calling you to do?
What circumstance has God arranged,
To help you bring a miraculous change?
For you are a child of God Most High,
And you may not always understand why,
There are so many things you go through,
But your problems may not be just for you.

~

So endure the trials, endure the pain,
God will use them to break the chains,
Of others who are watching your life,

Who do not know about Jesus Christ.

Perhaps bad situations will be uncovered,

And the power of God will be discovered,

By those who are hurting and feeling down,

By those who are chained and very bound.

And when you come forth with victory,

Maybe they will also be saved and set free.

So keep praying in all you go through,

Because your problems are not just for you.

****

Promises for Prayer

And he spake a parable unto them to this end, that men ought always to pray, and not to faint.

Luke 18:1

Praying always with all prayer and supplication in the Spirit, and watching thereunto with all perseverance and supplication for all saints.

Ephesians 6:18

And said unto them, Why sleep ye? rise and pray, lest ye enter into temptation.

Luke 22:46

Therefor I say to you, whatever things you ask when you pray, believe that you receive them, and you will have them.

Mark 11:24

The Lord is far from the wicked, but He hears the prayer of the righteous.

Proverbs 15:29

And all things, whatsoever ye shall ask in prayer, believing, ye shall receive.

Matthew 21:22

Thou shalt make thy prayer unto him, and he shall hear thee, and thou shalt pay thy vows.

Job 22:27

Pray without ceasing.

1 Thessalonians 5:17

Give ear, O LORD, unto my prayer; and attend to the voice of my supplications. In the day of my trouble I will call upon thee: for thou wilt answer me.

Psalm 86:6-7

The effectual fervent prayer of a righteous man availeth much.

James 5:16

And when you pray, do not be like the hypocrites, for they love to pray standing in the synagogues and on the street corners to be seen by others. Truly I tell you, they have received their reward in full. But when you pray, go into your room, close the door and pray to your Father, who is unseen. Then your Father, who sees what is done in secret, will reward you.

Matthew 6:5-6 (NIV)

When Paul and Silas sang and prayed,
Everyone's chains were loosened that day.

Be Thankful

And be ye thankful.
Colossians 3:15

Jesus healed ten leprous men one day, but only one man returned to say thank you. The man had to turn around from where he was going to come back and thank Jesus. It might have required a sacrifice on his part to show his gratitude, but he took the time to do it. The other nine men did not return. They went on their way and enjoyed their miraculous healing without personally thanking Jesus.

Have you ever gone out of your way to do something nice for someone, but the person did not acknowledge your special effort by saying thank you? Do you remember how you felt? When you see the Lord working in your life in an awesome way, when He begins to turn your situation around, do not forget to say "Thank you." As He blesses you each day, in the good times and bad, tell Him "Thank You." In every situation, find something for which you can thank God. He is always blessing you with His goodness.

In Your Life...

Do you thank God in everything?
Thank God for all of His goodness in your life. Thank Him for your spiritual blessings, materials blessings, physical blessings, family blessings, and much more. You should thank God for the big things that He does, as well as the little things.

Do you thank God for salvation?
Thank God for the salvation that He has given you through the precious blood of Jesus Christ. Ephesians 2:8 says, "For by grace are ye saved through faith; and that not of yourselves: it is the gift of God." What a very precious gift it is!

Do you thank God every day?
Each day that God gives you is a gift. Thank Him for every day – your life, health, and strength. No matter the problem that you may be facing today, things could always be worse. Look around and see how good God has been to you, and say, "Thank you, Jesus!"

Tell God "Thank you!"

Thank You

At midnight I will rise to give thanks unto thee
because of thy righteous judgments.
Psalm 119:62

As I see this brand new day,

I want to take this time to say,

Thank you, Lord, for all you've done,

I hear the birds, I see the sun.

It's one more day you've given me,

Filled with your grace and mercy.

From my heart, I want you to know,

I'm so glad you've blessed me so.

~

Thank you for your goodness and love,

And all your gifts sent from above.

You give your blessings graciously,

Thank you, Lord, for blessing me.

~

I know you healed ten lepers one day,

But only one returned to say,

"Thank you, Lord, for healing me,"
But the others left ungratefully.
Although you saved them from death,
And freely restored them to health,
They did not take the time to do,
One small thing – to say "Thank You."

~

You give me blessings from above,
And I am grateful for your love.
So "Thank you" is what I will say,
When I come to you and kneel to pray.

~

For every day, your love's the same,
And I have no reason to complain,
Though problems come and problems go,
But this one thing I surely know,
You give your blessings graciously,
So thank you, Lord, for blessing me.

****

Promises for Thankfulness

In every thing give thanks: for this is the will of God in Christ Jesus concerning you.

1 Thessalonians 5:18

Be careful for nothing; but in every thing by prayer and supplication with thanksgiving let your requests be made known unto God.

Philippians 4:6

At midnight I will rise to give thanks unto thee because of thy righteous judgments.

Psalm 119:62

And let the peace of God rule in your hearts, to the which also ye are called in one body; and be ye thankful.

Colossians 3:15

Remember his marvellous works that he hath done; his wonders, and the judgments of his mouth.

Psalm 105:5

O give thanks unto the LORD, for he is good: for his mercy endureth for ever.

Psalm 107:1

Enter into his gates with thanksgiving, and into his courts with praise: be thankful unto him, and bless his name.

Psalm 100:4

Rooted and built up in him, and stablished in the faith, as ye have been taught, abounding therein with thanksgiving.

Colossians 2:7

And I thank Christ Jesus our Lord, who hath enabled me, for that he counted me faithful, putting me into the ministry.

1 Timothy 1:12

But thanks be to God, which giveth us the victory through our Lord Jesus Christ.

1 Corinthians 15:57

Since we are receiving a Kingdom that is unshakable, let us be thankful and please God by worshiping him with holy fear and awe.

Hebrews 12:28 (NLT)

Therefore, let us offer through Jesus a continual sacrifice of praise to God, proclaiming our allegiance to his name.

Hebrews 13:15 (NLT)

You give your blessings graciously,
Thank you, Lord, for blessing me.

Be Peaceful

For it is God who works in you.
Philippians 2:13 (NIV)

God is calling you to a place of peace. Yes, you can have the peace of God today. Meditate on God's word and think about how He worked in the lives of people in the Bible. In the same way, God can guide and bless you. No matter how you feel, He understands what you are going through. In the midst of your situation, just depend on Him, trust Him, and honor Him with your life. As you keep looking up to Him, keep holding on to His word, and keep praising Him, you will find a peace that surpasses all understanding.

Decide that you will live each day for Jesus and be prayerful, thankful, and generous. When you do, He will bless you and make you a blessing. Then your life will be a story that you can share with others. Just like the people you have read about in this book, you will have a story to tell.

In Your Life…

God is working in your life.
Every person will have difficulties and challenges in life. Although each person's experiences are unique, your testimony can be a source of inspiration and encouragement to others who experience difficult situations. Share your testimony so other people can be motivated to trust God in their difficult situations.

Use your gifts and talents for God.
God has given you gifts and talents that are uniquely and genuinely yours. You can use them to bless the Kingdom of God in a way that no one else can.

You can bless others.
Whether through your life, testimonies, gifts, or service, you can be a blessing to others. As you walk with God, He will receive glory from your life and you will be a godly example for others who are following in your footsteps.

Live so God can get the glory,
Live and tell others your story.

Your Story

Let the redeemed of the LORD tell their story—
those he redeemed from the hand of the foe,
Psalm 107:2 (NIV)

The Word of God is faithful and true,
It's a book that was written just for you.
But the Bible is not where the story ends.
For in every life, God will begin,
To reveal himself and show you,
How He can work in your life too.

~

Hear His voice and heed His call,
And give to Him your all and all,
And live so God can have the glory,
Yes, live so you can share your story.

~

Write your story down on pages,
That others can read through the ages,
And see the things that you went through,
And how God worked them out for you.

****

Promises for You

Tell your children about it in the years to come, and let your children tell their children. Pass the story down from generation to generation.

Joel 1:3 (NLT)

Everyone will share the story of your wonderful goodness; they will sing with joy about your righteousness.

Psalm 145:7 (NLT)

This shall be written for the generation to come: and the people which shall be created shall praise the LORD.

Psalm 102:18

One generation shall praise thy works to another, and shall declare thy mighty acts.

Psalm 145:4

Let me proclaim your power to this new generation, your mighty miracles to all who come after me.

Psalm 71:18 (NLT)

Don't you realize that in a race everyone runs, but only one person gets the prize? So run to win!

1 Corinthians 9:24 (NLT)

But this one thing I do, forgetting those things which are behind, and reaching forth unto those things which are before, I press toward the mark for the prize of the high calling of God in Christ Jesus.

Philippians 3:13-14

But seek ye first the kingdom of God, and his righteousness; and all these things shall be added unto you.

Matthew 6:33

Look, I am coming soon! My reward is with me, and I will give to each person according to what they have done. I am the Alpha and the Omega, the First and the Last, the Beginning and the End.

Revelation 22:12-13 (NIV)

As long as it is day, we must do the works of him who sent me. Night is coming, when no one can work.

John 9:4 (NIV)

Write your story down on pages,
That others can read through the ages.

About the Great Peace Series for Christian Living

Finding Great Peace in the Word of God

The books in the *Great Peace Series for Christian Living* venture into the pages of the Bible and explore the lives of people just like you. In these books, you will learn how people with real problems experienced God in a real way during the difficult times of life. Each book includes biblical insights and inspirational poetry, as well as many pages of promises from the Word of God. Together, the Bible people, poetry, and promises will help you find the great peace that only God can give.

The Great Peace Series for Christian Living includes books for enduring the storms of life, beginning again, and facing each new day. The series also includes books written specifically for women, men, mothers, fathers, wives, husbands, parents, ministers, leaders, and more. Each book in the series has a companion journal that you can use to capture your personal thoughts and notes. Discover how you can find great peace in the Word of God through this series of inspirational books at www.GreatPeace.com.

ABOUT SHIRLEY D. HICKS

Shirley D. Hicks is a writer of Christian inspirational books and poetry. Her books in the *Great Peace Series for Christian Living* are a source of encouragement for people who are facing difficult and challenging times. After spending several years reading and studying the Bible, Shirley decided to pursue her passion for writing Christian books. Her writings have inspired and blessed many people. With bachelor's degrees in Computer Science and Math, Shirley spent more than fifteen years as an IT professional. She also has a master's degree in Theological Studies from Liberty University, Lynchburg, Virginia. She and her husband have one daughter. Visit her website at www.GreatPeace.com.

*Get the companion **Journal** to this book!*

The Great Peace for Today Journal includes encouraging excerpts from the *Great Peace for Today* book, plus one hundred pages for your journal entries. Get a copy today and write your story!

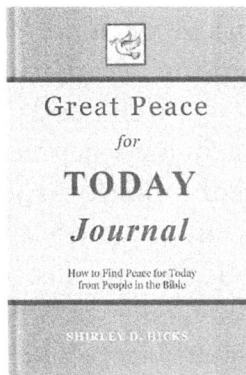

The Great Peace for Today
JOURNAL

Available at
www.GreatPeace.com

God Can Give a Mother Peace!

Great Peace for Mothers
How to Find Peace in Difficult Times
from Mothers in the Bible

Available in print and eBook at
www.GreatPeace.com

See all of the books in the

Great Peace Series for Christian Living

at

www.GreatPeace.com

www.ingramcontent.com/pod-product-compliance
Lightning Source LLC
Chambersburg PA
CBHW051043030426
42339CB00006B/174